Between day & night we rise

time travelers. Who isn't?
— Lu Reed

Credit goes to
poet LuCxeed,
and the team of designers,
photographers, and editors
at the publisher: D'Moon

Copyright ©D'Moon
first edition: 2022
all rights reserved
except for following public domain images:
fox (p85), sculpture (p86) and tombstone (p87)

ISBN: 978-1-933187-58-7

Slight variations may occur
as part of the print-on-demand process
since each book is manufactured in its entirety.

Your feedback is most welcome ~
publisher@worldculturepictorial.com

Selected LuCxeed Poems

Contents

Brief Beginning   2 - 3
    Between day and night we all are
    time travelers. Who isn't?

Copyright   4
Title   5
Contents   6 - 25

Quote from introduced poem
    in text   8 - 25
    in art calligraphy   26 - 45

Spirit Speed

Poem in art   46 - 107

Intrepid Legend   48 - 51
Spirit Speed   52 - 53
Road Untraveled   54 - 59
Gear Shift   60 - 63
His Backyard   64 - 65
Shield from More Love   66 - 69
Farewell   70 - 71
Sweet Bond   72 - 73
At Edge of Moonlight   74 - 79
To a Child Inside   80 - 81
Old Fox .i.   82 - 85
My Failure   86 - 89
Night   90 - 95
Song from Calm Sea   96 - 103
Who Isn't?   104 - 107

Selected LuCxeed Poems

Contents

"Dawn opens the magnificent gate
of its gigantic castle erected
into Heaven at the darkest
   dark night.
No noise. No sound.
Quiescence takes away
   the breath of Air,
calms impatient Wind."

Spirit Speed

Quote in art Calligraphy &
introduced poem title   26 - 27

"Like thunder over
    'Ocean of Fire'
Heat, death, hostility
    are nothing
Unbridled Spirit
    is bucking to win"

Selected LuCxeed Poems

Contents

"Lost the trace of return.
No sign of threading through.
A road untraveled
Traps me in nowhere.
I make two turns, finding no clue;
I make a third turn to think it through."

Spirit Speed

Quote in art Calligraphy &
introduced poem title

"Each road begins with a road
Untraveled, with the first march
Of a heedless hasty run,
Of a life-and-death escape,
Of a pioneer's courage."

Selected LuCxeed Poems

Contents

3

"He has a backyard
a rose garden
a marble yard
Name carved -
In Thought"

Spirit Speed

Quote in art Calligraphy & introduced poem title

"Chandelier overhead is haughty, champagne flute, snooty; candlelight seems intimidated, fluttering in, flittering out, unsteady."

Selected LuCxeed Poems

Contents

3

"Let's wing flowers with wind...
Let's call birds to slow down,
 to glide,
To perch, to dance outside
 your window.
Let's wake up the little kid,
 sleepy inside"

Spirit Speed

Quote in art Calligraphy &
introduced poem title

"Farewell
Our company
Every employee
...
Emptiness will haunt office
Farewell
A lost field
Once carrying our pride"

Selected LuCxeed Poems

Contents

3

"The moonlight descending
dims over the wilderland
Green eyes of wolves, greedy, blink
I hear the fear of trembling grass"

Spirit Speed

Quote in art Calligraphy &
introduced poem title

"The moonlight travels to
the metro
So I follow, into a deep street
where Dark refuses to retreat"

Selected LuCxeed Poems

Contents

3

"You like me, right? I know it
A pet cat's squinted eyes
A cute dolphin's perpetual smile
A dog's pleasing fairy tail"

Spirit Speed

Quote in art Calligraphy &
introduced poem title

"My head is as heavy
    as the stone
    as cold as the tomb
Buried beneath
    the cold stone tomb
    solemn
Is my heart, my joy
    my sunshine, my boy"

Selected LuCxeed Poems

Contents

"The world looks more real
as I perceive in daytime;
The world is obscure,
    blear, unreal,
as Night sedates
life's brain, abated,
to close eyes,
to sleep like the newborn
(or as the dead...)"

Spirit Speed

Quote in art Calligraphy &
introduced poem title

"I love longer daytime
(would you?)
...
modern fancy lights,
triple layers of curtains,
all pushing away dark Night
out of my sight -
yet eyes disobey..."

Selected LuCxeed Poems

Contents

"Laid over the blue
sway over the wave
tied to my boat to float
clouds buoyed up into the sky
imitate me and my boat
afloat
...hear music
from beneath
seemingly fish singing..."

Spirit Speed

Quote in art Calligraphy &
introduced poem title

"my lost True Love
near or afar
I left a long time ago
Still think of you
It is an unspoken fear
I left... sweet Love unshattered"

Selected LuCxeed Poems

Contents

"my lost Impossible Love
near or afar
I left a long time ago
Still think of you
It'll be a ruin to take care more
Than you can do. My hero"

Spirit Speed

Quote in art Calligraphy &
introduced poem title

"Wind blowing,
Star moving,
I traveling
out of night into daytime...
It's non-stop
as Time won't pause
between day and night,
between darkness and daylight."

Quote a poem to introduce the poem

quote "intrepid legend"
to introduce the poem

Dawn opens
the magnificent gate
of its gigantic
castle erected
into Heaven
at the darkest
dark night.
No noise, No sound.
Quiescence
takes away
the breath of Air,
calms impatient Wind.

quote "spirit speed"
to introduce the poem

like thunder over
"Ocean of Fire"
Heat, death, hostility
are nothing
Unbridled Spirit
is bucking to win

quote "road untraveled"
to introduce the poem

Lost the trace
 of return.
No sign of
 threading through.
A road untraveled
Traps me in nowhere.
I make two turns,
 finding no clue;
I make a third turn
 to think it through.

quote "road untraveled"
to introduce the poem

Each road
begins with a road
untraveled,
with the first step
Of a heedless, hasty run,
Of a life-and-death escape,
Of a pioneer's courage,

quote "his backyard"
to introduce the poem

He has
a backyard
a rose garden
a marble yard
Name carved –
In Thought

quote "gear shift"
to introduce the poem

Chandelier
overhead is haughty,
champagne flute,
snooty;
candlelight
seems intimidated,
fluttering in,
flittering out,
unsteady.

quote "to a child inside"
to introduce the poem

Let's wing flowers
 with wind...
Let's call birds
 to slow down,
 to glide,
To perch,
 to dance outside
 your window.
Let's wake up
 the little kid,
 sleepy inside...

quote "farewell"
to introduce the poem

Farewell
Our company
Every employee
...
Emptiness will
haunt office
Farewell
A lost field
Once carrying
our pride

quote "at Edge of Moonlight"
to introduce the poem

The moonlight
descending
dims, over
the wilderland,
Green eyes of wolves,
greedy, blink
I hear
the fear
of trembling grass

quote "at Edge of Moonlight"
to introduce the poem

The moonlight
travels to
the metro
So I follow,
into a deep street
Where
Dark refuses
to retreat

quote "old fox"
to introduce the poem

You like me, right? I know it
A pet cat's squinted eyes
A cute dolphin's perpetual smile
A dog's pleasing fairy tail

quote "my failure"
to introduce the poem

My head
is as heavy
as the stone
as cold
as the tomb
buried beneath
the cold
stone tomb
solemn
is my heart
my joy
my sunshine
my boy

quote "night"
to introduce the poem

The world
looks more real
As I perceive in daytime;
The world is obscure,
blear, unreal,
As Night sedates
Life's brain, abated,
To close eyes,
to sleep like the newborn.
(or as the dead...)

quote "night"
to introduce the poem

I love
longer daytime
(would you?)

modern fancy lights
triple layers
of curtains
all pushing away
dark night
out of my sight
yet eyes disobey....

quote "song from calm sea"
to introduce the poem

Laid over the blue
sway over the wave
tied to my boat to float
clouds buoyed up
into the sky
imitate me and my boat
afloat
...hear music
from beneath
seemingly fish singing
...

quote "song from calm sea"
to introduce the poem

"My lost True Love
near or afar
I left a long time ago
Still think of you
It is an unspoken fear
I left....sweet Love
unshattered"

quote "song from calm sea"
to introduce the poem

"my lost
Impossible Love
near or afar
I left a long time ago
Still think of you
It'll be a rain to
take care more
than you can do
my hero"

quote "who isn't"
to introduce the poem

Wind blowing
Star moving
travelling
out of night
into daytime

It's non-stop
as time won't pause
Between
day and night
Between darkness
and daylight

POEM

LuCxeed Poem
Intrepid

Dawn opens the magnificent gate
of its gigantic castle erected
into Heaven in the darkest
 dark night.
No noise. No sound.
Quiescence takes away the breath
of Air, calms impatient Wind.

Intrepid Legend

All in less than a blink,
bursts out Light, dilates, dilates,
as Ocean quakes,
    and shakes off dams;
breaks out an argentine
    White Steed,
immense, gallops, gallops,
bucking in the first daylight,

LuCxeed Poem

all in less than a blink,
neighing like deafening thunder,
front hooves kicking skyward,
silver mane blazing into air,
silence of Horizon shattered.
Prodigious. Brilliant. Intrepid.

Intrepid Legend

One of thousands of times.
    In a quiet-
filled moment when Night
    retreats, I wait
for the ever-punctual,
    my uttermost
loyal legend from
    the castle of Dawn,
to mount, to chase the rhythm
of Life. My White Steed,

TODAY is his name.

LuCxeed Poem

Spirit

Sunlight burns
    the deadly desert
Sandstorms
    gulp riders
In the long-distance
    3000-mile race
Flying through is
    a non-Arabian
        tiny horse

Spirit Speed

Like thunder over
  "Ocean of Fire"
Heat, death, hostility
  are nothing
Unbridled Spirit
  is bucking to win
I see in him the undefeated
  Spirit Speed

Road Untraveled

LuCxeed Poem

Road Untraveled

I'm in the middle
Of nowhere, of somewhere,
Led by a road untraveled.
Lost the trace of return.
No sign
       of threading through.
A road untraveled
Traps me in nowhere.
I make two turns,
       finding no clue;
I make a third turn
       to think it through.
Each road begins with a road
Untraveled,
       with the first march
Of a heedless hasty run,
Of a life-and-death escape,
Of a pioneer's courage.

LuCxeeд Poem

Road Untraveled

Each road takes shape
When being treaded through.
Each road marks
    a man's first march
In hopeless fear, or a pioneer
Who fears not, of nowhere
The untraveled road
    may wind up.
Each road takes shape
When being treaded through.
Each road marks
    a man's first march
In hopeless fear, or a pioneer
Who fears not
Of lurking snakes
Of crocodile in shoal
Of hunger, of thunder.

LuCxeed Poem

On such a road untraveled
I find myself –
Too late to find
Any trace of return.
Too soon to give up the trip.
I keep cool
To think it through –
No returning point.
No point to return.
Why not
    not to think of return?
Just to follow
    each first pioneer.
Involuntary,
    or a volunteer.
Just to move on the road
Untraveled, to tread through.

Road Untraveled

I am lured onto
    a road untraveled –
Life yearns to
    bask in audacious Nature,
To gallop into
    an unclaimed future,
To savor fruits
    of gutsy adventure,
To triumph over daring venture.
"March on. You'll be through."
No returning point. Move on.
Whatever it will be will be.
Don't fall amidst hazard
Though footprints will dazzle
In pride to pave a new road
From a road untraveled.
It is life. Don't fall. Think no more.
March on. I'll be through.

LuCxeeD Poem

60

Gear Shift

I'm not running
>on stadium ground,
nor in a ballgame,
>frolicking around,
instead, seated
in a fairly pricey
hub at the top of the city,
detailed in intricate luxury,
strictly observing formality.

LuCxeed Poem

Chandelier overhead
    is haughty,
champagne flute,
    snooty;
candlelight seems
    intimidated,
fluttering in,
    flittering out,
unsteady.
Red wine is fine.
White wine is fine.
Probably Scotch shifts
the gear inside.

Gear Shift

I feel I'm being
    dragged
down to the basement,
until my vision
    is surrounded
by gray cement, arid;
my imagination
    is half dead,
seeing but factual facts,
    solid,
though I'm still seated
in a fairly pricey
hub at the very
    top of the city,
smell and breathe luxury.

LuCxeed Poem
His Backyard

He has a backyard
a rose garden
a marble yard
Name carved –
   In Thought

He talked
   in a gentle tone –
"All hold stories
all shining in sunshine
teary on a rainy day
as Life rides tides

His Backyard

When I go
they too
are on the road
though
their home is my backyard"

IN THOUGHT

LuCxeed Poem

Shield from More Love

66

Shield from More Love

Love is Debt
So deep
I cannot
pay back

Affection
Attention
Obligation
Dedication

All in command
None to decease, to cease
until Earth kisses
the parting torment

LuCxeed Poem

Love is Debt
So deep
It takes Life
to pay back

I *shield myself
from more love
to pay back
Love inspiring my life*

In Love is in Debt
So deep
It takes Life
to pay back

LuCxeed Poem

Farewell
Everything must be gone
Every soul must be gone

Farewell
Our company
Every employee

Farewell
Dust is *always*
 demanding mess
Emptiness
 will haunt office

Farewell

Farewell
A lost field
Once carrying our pride

Farewell
We hugged, tears
   in eyes
"Take care!" "Goodbye"

LuCxeed Poem
Sweet

Every time I see
busy Bee
I see
silhouette
of sweet
Honey
Nectar
flowers' mystique
calling for Bee
"over here"

Sweet Bond

Bond

Yes, there goes
busy bee's
life journey

Sweet bond
made in Heaven –
Flower, Nectar
Bee, Honey

EuCxeeD Poem

At the Edge of Moonlight

At Edge of Moonlight

The moonlight
   is translucent
upon the translucent
icy world of ice
   crystal blue
freezing cool
   as I walk into

LuCxeed Poem

The moonlight
    descending
dims over the
    wilderland
Green eyes of wolves
    greedy, blink
I hear the fear
    of trembling grass

At Edge of Moonlight

The moonlight travels to
the metro
So I follow
    into a deep street
where Dark
    refuses to retreat

lurks in corners
hangs out in the bar
    smokes
Sidewalks are shelters
    for scared folks
nowhere else
    to go

Lucxeed Poem

Their eyes
    pleading at the foot
of buildings
    tall yet indifferent
Standing between me
and the Dark

where lies the edge
of the motionless
    moonlight
I hesitate
to go back
    to go ahead

At the Edge of Moonlight

LuCxeed Poem

To a Child Inside

To a Child Inside

Let's *wing flowers*
    with wind
To *fly, to waft, to clap*
    at your door;
Let's call birds to slow down,
    to glide,
To perch, to dance outside
    your window.

Let's *wake up the little kid,*
    sleepy inside,
To be once we were, lively,
    sunny, jolly.
Flower petals are capering,
    Bird eyes *winking* –
"Aren't you happy now,
    Child?"

Old Fox .i.

You like me, right?
    I know it
A pet cat's squinted eyes
A cute dolphin's
    perpetual smile
A dog's pleasing
    fairy tail

You like to see
what you want to see
You do not see
what you do
    not want to see

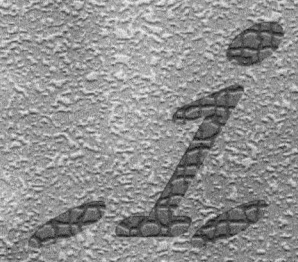

LuCxeeD Poem

An *apparent novice*
yet *ardent apprentice*
of *a veteran old fox*
    since
I, at all, am
    a descendent
    of ancestry

I *like you too,*
Why? You cannot
    guess
if *you do, I would*
feel sorry for myself

Old Fox .i.

It would be a shame
not to be a fox
    supposed to be –
supposed to be
    in disguise
as my master,
    an old fox,
        always is

My Failure

My head is as heavy
    as the stone
    as cold as the tomb
My silver hair touched
    by Sympathy
    in the moonlight
Buried beneath
    the cold stone tomb
    solemn
Is my heart, my joy
    my sunshine, my boy

LuCxeed Poem

I followed
    when he was toddling
    and giggling
I watched
    when he chased the ball
    kicking and skipping
I remembered
    every moment
    seeing him humming
    and growing
Yet I failed
    to protect him
    from the claws
    and prowl of guile

My Failure

My head is as heavy
   as the stone
   as cold as the tomb
My silver hair shone
   by hopeless moonlight
My hands
   writhe and hold
   the moist soil
My last voiceless cry
   is for my
   ever-departed boy

LuCxeeд Poem

Night

Night

The world looks more real
as I perceive in daytime;
The world is obscure,
    blear, unreal,
as Night sedates
Life's brain, abated,
to close eyes,
to sleep like the newborn
(or as the dead –
eyes shut, lie in bed,
see nothing,
feel nothing,
hear nothing).

LuCxeed Poem

Night

Night

I love longer daytime
(would you?)
to party on, or
have job done.
Faith
in modern fancy lights,
triple layers of curtains,
all pushing away
    dark Night
out of my sight –
yet eyes disobey,
refuse to be pleased.
I've tried, tried, tried,
not yet triumphant.

LuCxeed Poem

Outside dark Night,
inside white Night,
to avenge sleepless time,
join to sedate
Life's brain, abated,
to close eyes,
to sleep like the newborn,
or as the dead lie in bed.
Oddly, after waking up,
yesterday's stress,
troublesomeness,
seems long gone –
a new me!

Night

What have happened
at Night?
I ask the infinite sky.

LuCxeed Poem

Song from

Laid over the blue
sway over the wave
tied to my boat to float
clouds buoyed up into the sky
imitate me and my boat
afloat

calm sea

Song from Calm Sea

LuCxeed Poem

Song from Calm Sea

in the midst
of calm sea
I try not to fall asleep
yet hear music
from beneath
seemingly fish singing

"my lost True Love
near or afar
I left a long time ago
Still think of you
It is an unspoken fear
I left... sweet Love unshattered

LuCxeed Poem

my lost Wordless Love
near or afar
I left a long time ago
Still think of you
Time runs out
Till parting, we talk

my lost Impossible Love
near or afar
I left a long time ago
Still think of you
It'll be a ruin to take care more
Than you can do. My hero

Song from Calm Sea

my lost Innocent Love
near or afar
I left a long time ago
Still think of you
Fate did not tie the knot
Nor drive you out of my heart

my lost Young Love
near or afar
I left a long time ago
Still think of you
Different life pages we stand on
I guess. Sad to assume so

LuCxeed Poem

my lost Handsome Love
near or afar
I left a long time ago
Still think of you
Probably I should give up
All other friends because of you

my lost pure love
near or afar
Forgive a sensitive
   unworldly Soul
Left you a long time ago
Lonely in the sea
Still think of you"

Song from Calm Sea

I open my eyes, splash water.
I'm not in sleep
yet do hear fish sing
music from beneath
in the midst
of calm sea

Gentle white clouds aloft
buoyed up
shaped into a giant harp
Melodies play with strings
mimic singing fish's song
Must be salty water:
    my eyes wet

Who Isn't?

Wind blowing.
Star moving.
I traveling
out of night into daytime.

Each day,
I perceive myself to travel
between day and night,
between darkness and daylight.

It's non-stop
as Time won't pause
between day and night,
between darkness and daylight.

LuCxeed Poem

I perceive myself
 a life-long time traveler,
 everyday,
constantly traveling
 in the name
 of Time.

Fortunate midday and midnight
hint to those lost in the everyday's
non-stop traveling
 in the name
 of Time.

Yes, Time Traveler. We all are.
Who isn't?

www.ingramcontent.com/pod-product-compliance
Lightning Source LLC
Chambersburg PA
CBHW050857240426
43673CB00009B/274